A LINCOLNSHIRE RAILWAY CENTRE

A. J. LUDLAM

Published by the
Lincolnshire Wolds Railway Society

Lincolnshire is a county of immeasurable beauty with its many towns and villages that remain largely untarnished by the excesses of the modern age. One of the largest counties in England, yet it is so often bypassed and overlooked by the rest of the country.

In times past, the county was covered by a labyrinthine network of railway lines, each of which contributed to the growth of modern-day Lincolnshire. Sadly, too many of them were closed, both before, during and after the Beeching cutbacks, leaving towns like Louth, Mablethorpe, Horncastle and Woodhall Spa disenfranchised from the national rail network to their lasting detriment.

Local historian Alf Ludlam has compiled a unique series of books documenting just what has been lost from the county's fascinating rail network and which has for long been passed over by writers outside Lincolnshire. In so many ways, they form a 'Domesday Book' of Lincolnshire railways, a unique record of the transport treasures on steel wheels that once were and which should never be forgotten but brought back to life in print for all to appreciate again.

A man of many talents, Alf was so much more than a railway author. He was a founder member of the Grimsby & Louth Railway Preservation Society, the fundraising arm of the Lincolnshire Wolds Railway, that keeps alive a section of the Great Northern trunk route from Grimsby to London. It is to Lincolnshire's premier standard gauge heritage line that the proceeds from these books are being donated.

Robin Jones, Honorary President,
Lincolnshire Wolds Railway Society.

Ivatt Atlantics 990 and 251. During the early years of BR, a number of the preserved locomotives that still steamed were used on specials. During 1953, the two Ivatt Atlantics were used on two Doncaster Plant 100-year celebration trains. The train is stopped by Grantham's Yard signal box. Note the amazing signal gantry and all the photographers on the adjacent platform. *From the Great Northern Railway Society's collection.*

ISBN 978-0-9954610-2-4

The Lincolnshire Wolds Railway Society would like to thank Alf Ludlam and Phil Eldridge for giving their time to produce this publication; to the Great Northern Railway Society and in particular their Photographic Collections Officer for help with compiling information. Also to Paul Craig, Michael Vanns, Terry Henderson, M. G. Boddy, Leyland Penn, Mike Franklin, Les Nixon, Rod Blencowe, Tim Newcomb, Andrew Murray and David Enefer for their contributions, and to Allinson Print & Supplies for their support with the project.

Printed by Allinson Print & Supplies, Allinson House, Lincoln Way, Fairfield Industrial Estate, Louth, Lincolnshire LN11 0LS

Issue 1. Autumn 2018.

CONTENTS

Grantham was a Mecca for trainspotters in steam days and the **A4** **Pacifics** would have undoubtedly been 'top of the cops' for the young enthusiasts watching on the platform. **None-other than world record-holder 60022 'Mallard'** is in charge of the up **'Flying Scotsman'** awaiting the off, as classmate **60019 'Bittern'** retires to the shed. *A. J. Ludlam collection.*

Stirling 7ft single 37. Whilst the Stirling 8-foot singles are well known, few know that there were other types of single driving wheeled Stirling engines. No 37 was built in Doncaster works at the same time as No 1. It is a 7ft single which lasted as a main line passenger engine until 1905. Whilst no longer on top links after the 1880's, they were well used on sharply timed fast services. The picture is around 1894, because of the side chains at the front of the loco, it is likely to have had the Smith's simple brake gear at this time, the splashers have their original slots but closed by a plate. The loco has the later type of Stirling outside spring tenders. The location seems to be the Nottingham platform whilst behind the loco is a 6-wheeled full brake van. *R. S. Carpenter/P. Craig collection.*

A total of 53 Stirling 8ft singles were built during 25 years, and they were shedded at various points along the mainline. Until after 1896 the GNR did not have water troughs so changed engines every 100 or so miles. 771 was a Grantham loco built in 1884, and is shown being refuelled and watered ready for a trip. The tender is one of the Ivatt types, probably of the R22 type with 3,140 gallon water capacity. *R. S. Carpenter/P. Craig collection.*

INTRODUCTION

Grantham has always been an important place for travellers. It stands astride one of England's greatest highways, the Great North Road, as well as having a station on one of the country's most important main railway lines.

Interesting town centre buildings include two coaching inns - The George and The Angel & Royal - while the handsome spire of St Wulfran's church dominates the skyline. A feature of the church is its library of chained books, which date back to 1472.

Before 1066 Grantham belonged to Editha, Edward the Confessor's Queen. It was still a Royal Manor when the Domesday Book was compiled. King Edward IV made a grant for a grammar school in the first year of his reign and later gave the town its charter. During the English Civil Wars Oliver Cromwell distinguished himself on Gonerby Moor, outside the town.

The Great North Road was at its busiest during the 1800s. In 1826 there were more people running hotels and taverns in Grantham than were engaged in any other single trade. Daniel Defoe asserted that Grantham was famous for "the abundance of very good inns, some of which are fit to entertain persons of the highest quality". This, however, was soon to change as the new-fangled railways made their presence felt.

A delightful advertisement for the many and varied items of agricultural machinery bring produced by Richard Hornsby & Sons Spittlegate Iron Works in Grantham at the end of the 19th Century.

GRANTHAM AND LINCOLN BRANCH.

Miles from Grantham	DOWN	WEEK DAYS.																				SUNDAYS.		
		1	2	3	4	5	6	7	8	9	10	11	12	13	14	16	18	19	20			1	2	3
		Gds	Etys	Coal	Pss C	Etys	Gds.	Pass A	Pass.	Goods & Cl.	Pass	Exp. Pass.	Etys	Gds. & Cl.	Pss A	Pss.	Pass.	Exp. Pass	Pss A			Gds	Gds	Pas
	From		N. England, train 64, p. 6.	Nottnghm, train 21, page 127		N. England train 67 page 7.	Colwick, trn 23, p. 127.		Fris. only.	M			Colwick, tn. 61, page 127.	Colwick, tn. 55, p. 128.		D Sats only							Nottnghm, tn. 12, p. 120.	
		a.m	a.m.	a.m.	a.m	a.m.	a.m.	a.m.	a.m.	a.m.	a.m.	p.m.		p.m.	p.m	p.m.	p.m.	p.m.	p.m			a.m	a.m	p.m
...	GNTM gds. dp	4 20	...	...	..	8 15	.	...	...	10 35	...	—	When necessary.	...	...	...	...	.	...	.	...	4 15	...	...
	GNTM psr. ..	4 25	7 20	.	7 40	.	...	9 33	10 40	...	11 22	1 5		.	3 5	4 19	6 0	7 40	8 52	...	.	4 20	.	7 45
4¼	Barkstone	...	...	...	7 49	...	...	*	*	X	...	...		...	B	4 28	...	...	9 1	.	...	...	...	...
4½	*Barkstone E. jn. pass*	...	...	7 30	..	...	8 53	...	...	...	...	...	1 15	1 25	...	...	...	.	...	...	...	...	7 27	...
6¾	Honington arr.	4 45	.	7 35	.	.	9 0	.	.	10 55	.	E	...		...	...		* *	...	...	...	4 40	7 32	.
	Honington dep.	4 55	...	8 0	7 54	...	9 10	9 45	10 52	11 23	11 33	.	...	X	3 16	4 33	O	.	9 6	...	...	4 50	7 45	7 55
9¾	Caythorpe arr.	..	7 50	8 10	.	8 40	9 20	...	...	10 1132	...	...	1 30	...	...	...	.	...	...	...	...	...	.	...
	Caythorpe dep.			8 20	8 1	-		9 52	10 58	1155	11 40	∽ P		X	3 23	4 40	6 16	∽	9 13	...	...	.	...	8 3
12¼	Leadenham arr.		...	...	.			...	...	12 5	...	...		...	...	...	...	...	...	...	...	...	.	...
	Leadenham dep.		.	J	8 7			9 58	11 4	12 50	11 46	∽		X	3 29	4 46	6 22	V	9 19	...	...	.	...	8 9
16	Navenby arr.	Mondays excepted.	...	Mons. excepted.	..	When necessary.	Barkstone East arr. 8.37 a.m.	...	...	11 1 0	...	...	Barkstone East arr. 12.48 p.m.	...	...	...	...	...	...	...	...	...	.	...
	Navenby dep.		.	J	8 13			10 4	11 10	1 35	11 52	1 28		X	3 35	4 52	6 28	V	9 25	...	...		...	8 15
19	Harmston arr.		...	..	..			...	...	1 45	...	.		...	...	.	...	...	...	...	...	...	.	.
	Harmston dep.		.	J	8 19			10 10	11 16	1 57	12 58	...		X	3 41	4 55	6 34	.	9 31	...	...	.	...	8 21
20¾	Waddingtn arr.		...	..	...			...	...	2 2	...	...		..	...	...	...	...	...	...	...	...	.	...
	Waddingtn dep.		.	J	8 23			10 15	11 20	2 15	12 3	.		X	3 46	5 2	...	.	9 36	...	...	.	...	8 26
22	Brcbg bk sg arr.		...	...	...			...	...	2 20	...	...		Sats. only.	...	...	...	...	...	...	...	...	.	...
	Brcbg bk sg dep.		.	J	..			.	.	2 50	.	.			...	...	.	.	...	...	...	.	...	.
23	.. gas sg. arr.		...	...	...			...	...	2 55	...	...			...	...	...	...	...	...	...	...	.	..
	.. gas sg. dep.		.	X	.			.	.	3 15	.	.			.	...	.	.	...	...	...	.	...	.
—	LNCN T. arr.		...	...	8 29			10 21	11 26	—	12 9	1 39			3 52	5 8	6 43	8 12	9 42	...	...	...	.	8 32
—	LNCN P. dep.		.	...	8 30			10 23	11 28	.	12 11	1 41			3 53	5 10	6 44	8 13	9 44	...	...	.	—	8 33
24½	LNCN psr. arr.	5 40	...	9 5	8 32	...		10 25	11 30	...	12 13	1 42		2 55	3 55	5 12	6 45	8 15	9 45	...	...	6 35	.	8 35
25½	LNCN Hlms ..	5 45	.	9 10		.				3 30				3 0						...	..	6 40	8 30	
	To									Doncaster, train 34, page 109.														

Miles from Lincoln Holmes	UP.	WEEK DAYS.																			SUNDAYS.	
		1	2	3	4	5	6	7	8	9	10	11	12	13	14	15	18	19	20	21	1	2
		Gds.	Pass	Pass	Exp Pass	Pass A	Iron st'ne	Exp Pass	Iron stone.	Gs. & Coal.	Pass A	Pass A	Iron stne.	Pass A	Iron stne.	Pass H	Gds.	Gds.	Gds.	Pass.	Gds.	Pass
	From																Doncaster, Train 41, page 113.					
				Sats. only.								Fris. only.						Sats. excepted.	Sats. only.	Sats. only.		
		a.m	a.m	a.m.	a.m.	a.m.	a.m.	a.m.	p.m.	a.m.	p.m.	p.m.	p.m.	p.m.	p.m.	p.m.	p.m.	p.m.	p.m.	p.m.	a.m.	p.m.
¼	LINCOLN Hlms. dep.	12 30	.	...	.	...	.	...	...	11 35	...	...	...	...	...	...	8 20	10 20	10 30	..	12 30	...
	LINCOLN pass. ..	...	7 30	9 47	10 0	10 15	...	11 35	.	11 40	1 50	2 55	...	4 25		6 30	8 30	10 25	10 35	10 20	...	2 5
2¼	Bracebridge gas sg. arr.	Mondays excepted.	...	...	...	...	.	...	When necessary.	11 45	...	...	...	...	When necessary.	...	.		.	...	...	...
	Bracebridge gas sg. dep.		.	.	.	.	...	.		12 20	.	.	...	.		.	...		...	.	...	.
3¼	.. brick sg arr.		...	...	...	...	.	...		12 25	...	...	...	...		...	.	Will take mail bags Lincoln to Grantham	.	...	...	...
	.. brick sg dep.		.	.	.	.	...	.		12 50	.	.	...	.		.	—		...	.	...	.
4¾	Waddington .... arr.		...	...	...	...	.	...		12 55	...	...	...	...		...			.	...	...	...
	Waddington dep.		7 37	.	.	10 22	...	.		1 5	1 57	3 2	...	4 32		6 37	X		...	10 37	...	2 12
6¾	Harmston . . . . arr.		...	...	...	...	.	...		1 10	...	...	...	...		...			.	...	...	...
	Harmston dep.		7 41	.	.	10 26	...	∽		1 20	2 1	3 6	...	4 37		6 41	X		...	10 41	...	2 17
9¾	Navenby .... arr.		...	...	...	...	.	...		10 1 30	...	...	...	...		...			.	...	...	...
	Navenby dep.		7 46	10 1	∽	10 32	...	11 48		2 15	2 6	3 11	...	4 43		6 47	X		...	10 47	.	2 23
12¾	Leadenham . . . arr.		...	...	...	...	.	...		2 25	...	...	...	...		...			.	...	...	...
	Leadenham dep.	...	7 54	10 7	∽	10 40	...	∽	.	2 55	2 14	3 18	...	4 51		6 54	X		...	10 54	...	2 31
15¾	Caythorpe .... arr.	...	...	...	.	...	.	...	...	3 5	...	...	...	...		...			.	—	...	...
	Caythorpe dep.	...	8 1	10 13	∽	10 47	11 0	∽	12 40	3 20	2 21	3 26	4 40	4 58	6 23	7 1	X	.	..	11 1	...	2 38
18¾	Honington . . . arr.	1 16	...	...	...	...	...	.	...	3 30	...	...	...	...	...	...	9 10	11 10	11 20	...	1 16	...
	Honington dep.	1 30	8 9	10 19	.	10 55	...	...	.	3 40	2 29	3 34	.	5 6	...	7 9	9 20	11 20	11 30	...	1 30	2 45
20¾	*Barkstone east jun. ... pass*	1 36	...	10 23	...	...	11 15	.	12 55	...	...	...	4 55	...	6 43	...	...	...	...	...	1 36	...
21	Barkstone . . . . . dep.	...	8 14	...		11 2	...		...	.	2 34	3 39	.	5 11	...	7 14	...	.	...		...	
25½	GRANTHM pas. arr.	.	8 22	.	1040	11 10	.	12 11	.	...	2 42	3 47	...	5 19	.	7 22				11 18	.	2 58
	GRANTHM gds ..	...		...			...		...	4 0					...		9 40	11 45	11 55		...	
	To	Nottingham, tn. 6, p. 121		Nottingham, trn 42, p. 121			Ardsley, tn. 213, p. 15.		Doncaster, train 300, page 18.				Colwick, tn. 77, p. 125.		Colwick, tn. 92, p. 128.					Will take mail bags from Lincoln to G'nt'm	Nottinghm, tn. 4, p. 120	

A May take cattle if wagons are fitted with brake pipes. See special instructions.
B Stops when required to take up passengers.
C One vehicle only conveying goods may be taken at rear, but there must be a brake vehicle *last*, in which guard must ride. May take cattle on Tuesdays from intermediate stations to Lincoln, if wagons are fitted with brake pipes. See special instructions.
D May convey cattle from beyond Grantham.
E Stops when required to leave first-class passengers.
H Meat wagon to be attached at Lincoln for meat from intermediate branch stations to London, also may take cattle, if wagons are fitted with brake pipes. See special instructions.
J Stops to leave wagons only. May take on important traffic.
M Load from Grantham not to exceed 25 wagons, to follow 8 down from Grantham on Fridays.
O Stops when required to leave passengers from Nottingham or take up for Lincoln.
P Stops on Thursdays to leave shop assistants from Grantham.
V Stops when required to leave passengers from Sleaford branch stations, and from Grantham and stations beyond.

THE ARRIVAL OF THE RAILWAYS

The Great Northern Railway (GNR) and the Ambergate, Boston, Nottingham & Eastern Junction Railway received their Royal Assents on 26 June and 16 July 1846 respectively. The Boards of the two companies began to discuss joint working at Grantham, and an Act of 22 July, 1847 cleared the way for a joint station in the town. The only section of the Ambergate company's railway ever to be completed was the 22 miles between Nottingham and Grantham. The Ambergate was the first company to enter Grantham, on 15 July, 1847.

The first station was located at Canal Yard, near the Nottingham & Grantham Canal basin. Intermediate stations were at Sedgebrook, Bottesford, Elton, Aslockton, Bingham and Radcliffe. Sidings and a warehouse were at Colwick. Four passenger services were worked each day on weekdays with two on Sundays. The line was double and there were earthworks near Gonerby where a tunnel passed through deposits of unstable blue clay.

In 1851 nearly 2,000 men were employed on railway construction in the Grantham area. The majority of these were classed as labourers, but there were large numbers of bricklayers, also miners, blacksmiths, carpenters and masons. Many who had moved to the area for work brought their families with them and most lived in accommodation provided by their employers. Most of the locally recruited men were former farm workers, who could earn far in excess of what they would do working on the land.

On 2nd August, 1852, Ambergate company trains began to use the joint station at Grantham, and Canal Yard station was relegated to goods-only on the same day. On this day the GNR advertised a through service between London and Nottingham via Grantham in less time than that offered by the London & North Western Railway and Midland Railway route. When the first train, with a through carriage from the 11.00 am train ex-King's Cross headed by a GNR engine, drew into Nottingham station the Midland officers, who regarded the arrival as defiance of the injunctions, used a number of Midland engines to force the GNR engine into the disused Midland Counties Railway shed. Once inside, the rails leading to the shed were lifted. The GNR initiated proceedings against the MR for stealing its engine. The court, however, stated that the MR was entitled to remove any locomotive that was 'wrongfully encumbering their lines'. They ignored the fact that the engine was legitimately hired by the Ambergate company and was crewed by its men.

The MR applied for powers to prevent the Ambergate railway company or the GNR using GNR engines on the Nottingham line and an injunction was allowed preventing the Ambergate company from running engines over the MR line until their fitness had been certified. The locomotives in use at the time were excluded from this restriction, except for two engines, one of which had caused the trouble.

A Class J3 coming into Grantham station from the Southern end, passing the Malting works. This style of locomotive was an evolution of the standard Stirling 0-6-0 which dated back to 1873. After Stirling died in 1895, a number of this standard design were still on order, whilst Ivatt also had a considerable number built from 1896 until 1901. Many were built at Doncaster but a number were also built by outside contractors such as Dubs and Co, which later became part of the North British Loco Company. Many of the earlier ones had been rebuilt by Ivatt with larger domed boilers, and in many cases the new style of cab. After Gresley was appointed Locomotive Engineer of the GNR, he started to rebuild many of the later locomotives with bigger, 4ft 8in dia boiler, domed, and with the Ivatt style cab. A number survived into BR times, but all had gone by 1954. Although the loco does not show a visible number, the Howlden style 45ft carriages in the train behind suggest the picture is post grouping (1923). *From the Great Northern Railway Society's collection.*

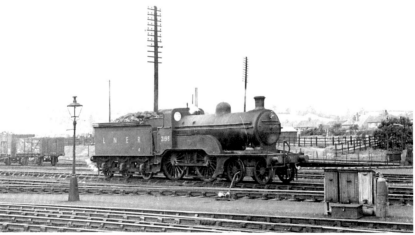

Class D2 4-4-0 2198 at Grantham on 8th July 1948. Allocated at Colwick, it was condemned soon after on 27th August that year. *H. C. Casserley/A. J. Ludlam collection.*

4

The Midland Railway refused to accept Nottingham parcels and any goods for destinations beyond Grantham. Through goods traffic to Nottingham began in August 1852 but had to be carted from Colwick. Passenger traffic continued to work into Nottingham; the Ambergate company held indisputable rights for its own locomotives.

The warfare at Nottingham was brought to a close by an agreement on 24th May, 1853, for the division of competitive traffic to four more towns, giving the GNR the following percentages.

	Passengers	Goods
Nottingham	50%	30%
Newark	80%	55%
Stamford	70%	30%
Peterborough	90%	33%

On 31st July, 1854 the Ambergate company obtained an Act allowing it to agree with the GNR to work the line and sell their rolling stock to them. A new station was opened in Nottingham on 3rd October, 1857 and the rental of the MR station ended. The new station was called London Road.

On 15th May, 1860 the Ambergate Company changed its name to the Nottingham & Grantham Railway & Canal Company. The following year the GNR started to lease the company, which was continually extended until the 1923 Grouping when the Nottingham & Grantham Company finally lost its nominal independence.

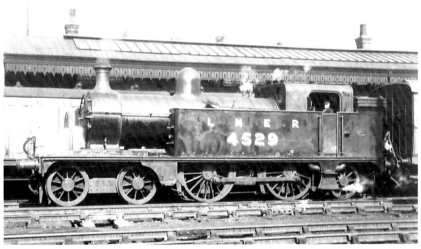

Ivatt Class C12 4-4-2T 4529 on station pilot duties at Grantham in April 1936. The locomotive was built at Doncaster in October 1901 and spent all its working life at Grantham. It received its BR number 67382 in 1949 and was withdrawn in April 1955. *A. J. Ludlam collection.*

Ivatt Class J1 65007. A total of 15 locomotives were introduced by H. A. Ivatt in 1908, which were originally designed to work fast goods trains with fitted brakes that the GNR was developing at that time. Built to one works order at Doncaster they were later seen on passenger trains, and should be more correctly called mixed traffic locomotives. They were the first class of GNR 0-6-0's to have larger coupled wheels at 5ft 8in, and were built without superheaters, remaining so until scrapped. Ivatt was a great believer in the advantages of standardisation and thus the boiler, wheels and motion were the same as that on his 0-6-2T N1 class. The loco shown in the photo was scrapped in 1952 and the final one in 1954. Moving away from Grantham, the loco is carrying stopping/suburban train headlamps. The home depot 'Colwick' is painted on the buffer beam. The five-carriage train is a typical mixture of pre-grouping and very modern Thompson steel sided non-corridor vehicles. *From the Great Northern Railway Society's collection.*

Class C1 4-4-2 No. 4408 pictured at Grantham in April 1936. 4408 was built in July 1905 and had a life of only 40 years, being withdrawn on 26th July, 1945. *A. J. Ludlam collection.*

Ivatt Atlantic 62822 under repair in the loco yard at Grantham. At the time, there was no wheel drop inside, hence the need for the rather crude lifting equipment which allowed the engine to be raised to remove the 6ft 8in dia driving wheels which are seen in front of the locomotive, along with the bogie and its wheels. The locomotive is still attached to the shear legs and supported by baulks of timber, which seem to be double the size of track sleepers. It is not clear what repairs are going on, however it seems likely that the driving wheel bearings were being attended to. 62822 was shedded at Grantham from 1947 until 1950. *From the Great Northern Railway Society's collection.*

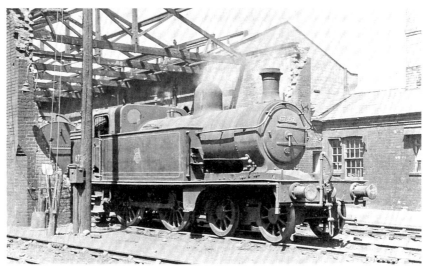

Grantham Class C12 4-4-2T 67352 standing outside the derelict entrance of the original shed building on 9th July, 1958. Condemned on 19th November that year, 67352 was the only member of the class to acquire the later BR emblem. *P. Groom/A. J. Ludlam collection.*

Grantham Class D1 4-4-0 3043 in the shed yard in April 1936. Built at Doncaster works in April 1909, 3043 remained a Grantham loco until it was withdrawn in June 1938. *A. J. Ludlam collection.*

C12 4529 on a shed road at Grantham. There were a total of 60 of the Ivatt 4-4-2Ts, with 50 of this type with rounded corners to the water tanks, built at Doncaster as suburban passenger engines in the period from 1898 to 1907. This particular locomotive was built in 1901 and had condensing gear to allow working on the Metropolitan Widened Lines in London. The condensing gear was removed in 1921, as this class of locos was replaced in the London area with other types. After grouping Grantham had as few as two of this type on shed, or as many as six depending on the turns required. This loco was scrapped in 1955 as **BR No. 67382.** *P. Craig collection.*

It was a further five years after arrival of the Ambergate company before the GNR began its services to Grantham, when the last section of its main line was opened between Peterborough and Retford on 1st August, 1852. The new Grantham station was designed by Goddard and built by the Sleaford firm of Kirk & Parry during 1852.

The northern extent of the main line from Grantham contrasted to its southern entry, which was mainly through cuttings. Going north the line made a sweeping curve over a short viaduct and then along an embankment past Barrowby Road signal box. It straightened out and crossed the Nottingham Road and the Great North Road. Not until it was adjacent to the village of Great Gonerby, over half a mile beyond Grantham station, did it enter the cutting to Peascliffe tunnel.

The GNR's Board of Directors did not rate Grantham as a place of importance until, in 1862, Archibald Sturrock got them to agree to the installation of engine pits and water cranes at Peterborough station, thus enabling engines

(16)
Great Northern Railway
TO
GRANTHAM

to run through from King's Cross to Grantham. This immediately changed the status of Grantham and a 40ft turntable was installed there in June 1862. Sturrock then made further requests for increased accommodation for engines in the town. He calculated that by working locomotives through to Grantham via Peterborough the GNR could make savings of £2,000 per annum. The old carriage shed was converted to an engine shed and a new carriage shed and sidings were provided at a cost of £1,500. The increased importance of Grantham's engine shed resulted in accommodation being provided for the Locomotive Foreman, the Inspector of Way and seventeen of the Locomotive & Traffic Department staff in 1866.

In November 1865 the down platform at Grantham station was extended. The new carriage shed survived this alteration but its reprieve was short-lived and it was removed when further works to the platform took place in the mid-1870s.

Messrs Kirk & Parry reconstructed the buildings on both platforms in 1878. Later a pair of new lines were laid, each 40 chains long, on the west side for Nottingham branch traffic between new signal boxes at Grantham North and Barrowby Road, where the branch diverged. A new ticket platform was brought into use in August 1882 whilst in 1886 a new bay platform was completed in March. A 50ft lengthening of the up platform was finished a month later. High Dyke signal box, for up traffic only, was opened in June 1882 when the slow line from Grantham was extended from Great Ponton.

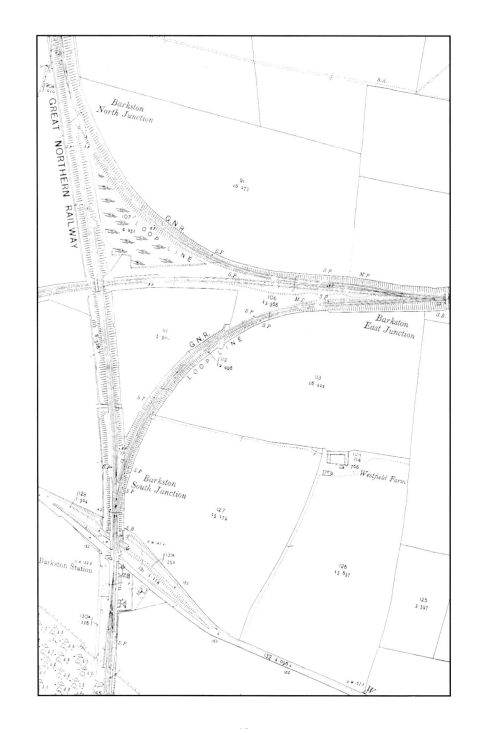

GREAT NORTHERN RAILWAY

Barkston
North Junction

G.N.R.
L O O P L I N E

G.N.R.
L O O P L I N E

Barkston
East Junction

Barkston
South Junction

Barkston Station

Westfield Farm

91
18·273

107
4·251

106
13·368

111
5·50,

112
2·496

113
16·222

114
·756

127
15·179

126
13·657

125
3·597

128
·504

130A
·116

131A
·350

132 4·026

160

163

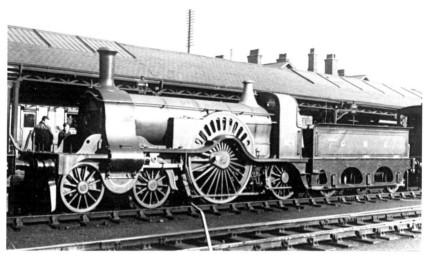

To celebrate the 100th anniversary of the GN main line from King's Cross to Doncaster, BR had a display of preserved engines and carriages at King's Cross. These included No 1, a Stirling 8ft single, pictured here in the bay at Grantham. It will be noticed that the connecting rod from the 8ft Driving wheel to the cylinders is missing. It was practice when moving locos not in steam to remove the connecting rod to ensure that the cylinders were not damaged by not being lubricated. The Stirling single is one of the most famous ex-GNR locomotives, and the first of a class of 53 locomotives built between 1870 and 1894. The class had been built to work trains of 150 tons behind the tender, at an average speed of about 51 mph between stops. The design of the tender was such that water could only be refilled at a station and Grantham, being 105 miles from London, was an ideal place for the locomotive to be exchanged. *From the Great Northern Railway Society's collection.*

The same locomotive today, posing on the turntable at York Museum. *P. Eldridge*

Class A3 Pacific 60065 'Knight of Thistle' on an up express at Little Ponton on 9th September, 1962. A New England-based example fitted with German smoke deflectors, 60065 was withdrawn on 28th June, 1964. *L. Nixon.*

THE RACE TO THE NORTH

When Grantham shed became an engine-changing point the early Hawthorn and Sharp locomotives would have been joined by the Sturrock and Stirling 2-4-0s and 0-4-2s. From 1871 the famous Stirling 8ft Singles were very much in evidence with No 2 the first to arrive. Variety was achieved when the GNR/MS&LR engine changeover point was moved from Retford to Grantham in 1883 for the working of the Manchester to King's Cross trains.

From 1st June, 1876 the 'Special Scotch Express' was timed to accomplish the journey between King's Cross and Edinburgh in nine hours. The up train departed from King's Cross at 10.00am and the overall speed from there to York was 47 mph. For the first time trains ran non-stop between King's Cross and Grantham - 105 miles in 130 mins. As the class of 8ft Singles grew in numbers, it was found a larger tender was more useful for faster running. This was the first regular 100 mile non-stop run in the country and remained so for ten years. The 10.10am third-class train was allowed only ten hours from King's Cross to Edinburgh from the same date.

During 1887/88 the West Coast and East Coast main line railway companies were fiercely contesting the race to Edinburgh. At first GNR men were reluctant to race, due to the premiums they could earn by economical running, but once they entered the spirit of things they were getting their trains to York in 3½ hours, the best time being 3hr 22mins on 21st August, 1888. Whereas the other companies confined working the 'Flyers' to one or two engines, which they kept in premium condition, the GNR used no less than ten different Stirling 8ft 4-2-2s and 7ft 2-2-2s during the racing. This reflected great credit on the design and maintenance of the locomotives and the capabilities of the enginemen. The 7ft 2-2-2 No 233 claimed 'even time' for the 105 mile run from King's Cross to Grantham on 25th August, 1888.

At the end of August the East Coast and West Coast main line railway companies came to a formal understanding that the overall schedule to Edinburgh by both routes should be 8½ hours. This came into force on 1st September, 1888. The night Scotch expresses in the summer of 1896 were the best scheduled GNR trains to Scotland and their timings were not surpassed until 1932. The Aberdeen train left King's Cross at 8.15pm and the timing to Grantham was 114mins (55mph), while that from Grantham to York was 88mins (56mph). The train arrived in Newcastle in five hours, Edinburgh in 7hrs 25mins, and Aberdeen in 10hrs 20mins.

Three clerestory carriages and at least one 12-wheeled bogie underframe shown early the following morning, with the post-crash fire still burning. *From the Great Northern Railway Society's collection.*

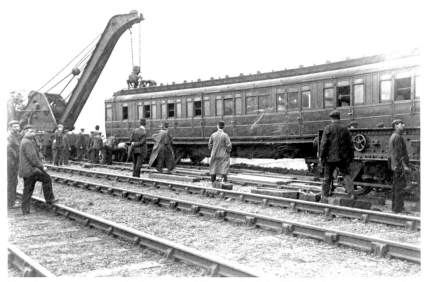

This picture shows one of the less damaged Clerestories being lifted back on to the track. It is suggested that the man in the centre with the lighter raincoat and bowler hat is **Nigel Gresley**, who was made **GNR Carriage and Wagon Superintendent in 1905.** The other two men to his left are obviously management, but we do not know who. The crane is being attached to the roof to complete the lifting. *From the Great Northern Railway Society's collection.*

THE 1906 ACCIDENT

On 19th September, 1906 Ivatt Large Atlantic No 276, with Driver F. W. Fleetwood and Fireman R. Talbot in charge, left King's Cross with the 8.45pm night Scotch express to Edinburgh Waverley.

The through Sleeping Car and Mail train was due at Grantham at 10.57pm. The signals were up, but people on the platform were horrified to see the train approach the station travelling at between 50mph and 60mph. An up goods train from the Nottingham line had just come over the junction and as the signalman was expecting the express to stop, he still had the points for the down Nottingham line in place. The speeding express ran first over a 10 chain left-hand curve and then on a 6.6 chain right-hand curve - too much for the tender, which derailed, broke away, and fell down the embankment. The engine keeled over on to its side.

The carriages, except the last four, were thrown all over the place with several down the embankment, and were badly damaged. At least two fires broke out amongst the wreckage. The driver, the fireman, nine passengers and a post-office worker were killed instantly. Two passengers later died from their injuries, and thirteen passengers and four railwaymen were injured.

Locomotive Superintendent, Henry Ivatt, came down from Doncaster straight away and could find nothing wrong with the engine. At the inquest no satisfactory explanation for the incident could be found.

The driver was an experienced man and had, in fact, driven the same train with the same engine, the previous two evenings. The fireman was an ex-Doncaster Premium Apprentice who had been promoted to work under the District Locomotive Superintendent.

Many explanations were put forward, such as the driver going mad, being drunk, taken ill or having a fight with the fireman. The evidence of the signalman at Grantham was that he had seen both men standing looking forward through the cab front windows, apparently calmly.

One possibility is that the driver had a seizure and the inexperienced fireman did not realise until too late.

Further investigation into the crash suggests that when the engine was changed at the previous stop of Peterborough, the vacuum hose was not connected properly, which made the brakes inoperative. This would not have been noticed on the climb from Peterborough and would have only become apparent when the brakes were applied as the train approached Grantham.

A1 60113 'Great Northern' was the original Gresley Pacific built for the GNR in 1922. It was one of many A1's that was not converted to the A3 type that, for instance, Flying Scotsman was. After a decent career on top notch trains, it was sent to Doncaster for major repairs, where Edward Thompson, the New Locomotive Engineer who took over from Gresley in 1941, decided to use this iconic locomotive as the prototype for his proposed class A1/1. This caused much consternation to many Gresley enthusiasts who felt the beauty of the original design had been destroyed by the rather ungainly modifications made to remove the inside motion and use the Thompson style valve gear. The footplate in particular lost its attractive lines. The locomotive has obviously been worked very hard recently, since the smokebox has a very visible 'hot spot'. It is not easy to distinguish the carriages on the train, but some do appear to be in 'Blood and Custard' livery. *From the Great Northern Railway Society's collection.*

Class A4 Pacific 4483 'Kingfisher' with an up express at Grantham in the 1930s. It had the distinction of working the final revenue-earning service for an A4 on the 0825 Glasgow-Aberdeen return trip on 14th September, 1966. *G. F. Gillford.*

Class C12 67397 was one of the batch built in 1907 and had its condensing gear removed in 1922. This loco had an interesting career after leaving London. After Grouping, it was sent up to the North Eastern Area and mainly shedded at Hull Botanic Gardens from 1930-54. It was the last surviving C12 and interestingly spent its last four years at Grantham, before being scrapped in December 1958. The loco appears to be shunting empty carriage stock of the Gresley type. *P. H. Groom/P. Craig collection.*

Ivatt D2 4-4-0 2180. This photo is post 1946, when the whole of the LNER loco stock was renumbered. As so often with photos of locos at Grantham it appears to be in the Nottingham platform and behind the tender is a Gresley 61ft 6in brake. The loco having been built in 1901 was scrapped before receiving its BR number in 1950. The D2 was the second class of Ivatt 4-4-0's built for the GNR, and were the prime main line express locomotives for many years until the Atlantics arrived in goodly numbers. After Grouping, they still worked main line trains, but after 1932, when more Pacifics were available they were sent off to country branches, whilst for some time, a number were stored. *H. C. Casserley/P. Craig collection.*

Ivatt Atlantic 62822 was the last of the class in revenue service. In November 1950, plans were laid to send it for scrapping. However, somewhere in BR, there was a manager with a heart, and he allowed the loco to work an enthusiast's excursion called the 'Ivatt Atlantic Special' between King's Cross and Doncaster on Sunday 26th November. The 9-carriage train included two ex-GC Kitchen cars and weighed 330 tons gross. The crew and Inspector were all carefully chosen due to their experience with the Atlantics. Although fog tried to spoil the day, by the time the train moved through Peterborough, and Grantham, it was clear enough to see the shed crews lined up to pay their last respects to these powerful passenger engines that had lasted 45 years in traffic. When the train arrived at Doncaster, a presentation was made to the son of H. A. Ivatt, H. G. Ivatt who was the last Locomotive Superintendent of the LMS, of one of the works plates from 62822, whilst the footplate crew were presented with a framed photo of the loco. 62822 was taken directly to the plant where it was later scrapped. *From the Great Northern Railway Society's collection.*

Class A4 Pacific 4496 in Grantham shed yard in 1946. Formerly named 'Golden Shuttle', she was re-named 'Dwight D. Eisenhower' after the United States General of the Army in February 1946. *G. F. Gillford.*

MOTIVE POWER

By 1895, of the fifty engines based at Grantham twenty-three of these were Singles of various types. From 1910 Singles were being replaced by Ivatt 4-4-0s, and only three Singles were left working from Grantham. Seven 'E1' class 2-4-0s were working local trains to Derby, Nottingham and Stafford by the Grouping in 1923. In 1915, seven Ivatt 'D1' 4-4-0s were stationed at Grantham working secondary routes to Boston, Leicester, Derby, Skegness and Mablethorpe. They also had some mainline duties, particularly in the York direction.

At the Grouping in 1923 the first three Gresley Class 'A1' Pacifics arrived to join over a quarter of the 93 existing Ivatt large-boilered Atlantics. The new A1s arriving at Grantham shed after 1923 included No's 1476 Royal Lancer, 1479 Robert the Devil, 1480 Enterprise, 2543 Melton, 2547 Doncaster, 2548 Galtee More, 2550 Blink Bonny, 2551 Prince Palatine, 2556 Ormonde, 2557 Blair Athol and 2558 Tracery. In 1926 the Gresley 'A1' Pacifics took over Grantham shed's Top Link working Grantham-York-King's Cross-Grantham or reverse - and after 1930 they were permitted to work the major London to Leeds workings. Grantham's shed facilities were never sufficient to be able to cope with the size and weight of the Pacifics. When they arrived the smoke vents in the roof of the 1899 shed had to be lifted to clear their cabs.

By the end of the 1930s Gresley 'V2' class 2-6-2s were at Grantham and from 1946 four Thompson Class 'B1' 4-6-0s were there, a number that remained constant until the 1960s. A former Great Eastern Railway Class 'B12' 4-6-0 was used on trains to Skegness, Peterborough and also on the Doncaster 'Parliamentary' workings during the British Railways period. The various 'J' class 0-6-0s were well represented, working slower passenger trains and goods traffic. Class 'J6' were prominent, eleven of them were stationed at Grantham in 1933 along with eight Class 'J3s'.

By nationalisation in 1948 most of the important duties were being performed by the Gresley Class 'A4' Pacifics, the first of which appeared in 1938. The streamliners worked the 'Flying Scotsman' non-stop to Newcastle. Grantham kept one engine of the class in superb condition for the duty and No 60030, Golden Fleece, was a regular. Secondary duties were carried out by Class 'K2' 2-6-0s.

In the early British Railways days Grantham shed received a batch of new Peppercorn 'A1' Pacifics, the first being No's 60117 Bois Roussel, 60133 Pommern, 60148 Aboyeur and 60149 Amadis. By the end of 1956 the 'A1' Pacific allocation peaked at twelve engines and they worked expresses such as the down 'Flying Scotsman', 'The Aberdonian' and 'The Tynesider' in addition to the up 'Northumbrian' and 'Heart of Midlothian'.

The introduction of through-running between King's Cross and Newcastle saw engines of the class transferred to other depots.

Class J52 0-6-0ST 4217 on shunting duties at Grantham in April 1936. Built between 1892 and 1901, there were originally 137 locomotives in the class. The last survivor was withdrawn in 1961 but 68846 has been preserved and restored in its **GNR** livery as No. 1247. *A. J. Ludlam collection.*

Class J4 0-6-0 4107 alongside **Grantham** station in **LNER** days. This loco was originally built by Dubs & Co in 1899 as part of the 315 series of transitional 0-6-0's between the original Stirling designs which went back to 1868, and the newer Ivatt style such as the J5 or J1/2 and 6. It was built with an Ivatt style cab and a domed boiler, and without the striking brass safety valve cover that was typically Stirling. It was originally **GNR** class J5 and later **LNER** J4. It was not ever rebuilt to a 4ft 8 boiler, rather retaining it original sized 4ft 5 one. It started life as GNR 1107, becoming 4107 after **Grouping** in 1923. It stayed as a J4 and made it through **World War 2** to be renumbered as 4121 in the 1946 system. Although it was allocated the **BR** number 64121, it seems clear it did not actually get painted with that number before it was scrapped in **November 1950**. *N. Stead collection.*

The 1906 Accident at Grantham

To our modern eyes it might seem macabre, but a series of postcards were produced of the aftermath of the 1906 accident and its clearing up. Apart from the Driver and Fireman there were another 12 deaths, including some who died after being rescued from the wreckage. This scene shows the beginning of the post-accident clean up with the crane already on site. There are two clerestory carriages on the left. *From the Great Northern Railway Society's collection.*

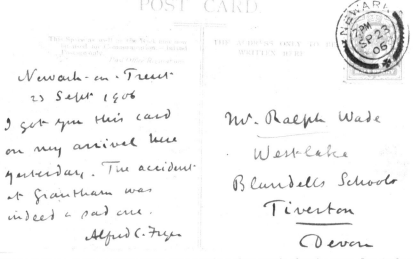

The back of one of the postcards which were sent by various people after the event. *From the Great Northern Railway Society's collection.*

York-based Class A1 Pacific 60125 'Scottish Union' on an up express at Little Ponton in July, 1963. One of four of the class to enter traffic in 1949, she had a life of only 15 years and was withdrawn twelve months after this picture was taken. *L. Nixon.*

Deltic D9016 in its original livery with an up express for King's Cross at Little Ponton in August, 1962. D9016 (later 55016) came into service on 27th October 1961 and was based at Haymarket depot. It was named 'Gordon Highlander' at Aberdeen in July 1964. Withdrawal came in December 1981 but it is one of six of the class that survived into preservation. *L. Nixon.*

Deltic 55015 'Tulyar' approaches Peascliffe tunnel with the 0933 Hull-King's Cross on 10th August, 1981. The Deltics were allocated to Finsbury Park, Gateshead and Haymarket depots. The Finsbury Park contingent were all named after famous racehorses, whereas the Gateshead and Haymarket examples bore the names of British Army Regiments in the North East of England and Scotland. *L. Nixon.*

Class 55 55022 'Royal Scots Grey' emerges from Peascliffe tunnel with a down express on 25th July, 1978. *L. Nixon.*

Class 20 20063 and 20071 approach Barkston East Junction with a Summer Saturdays only Leicester to Skegness service on 10th August, 1981. It was common to find Class 20s paired together at the nose with their cabs at opposite ends, ensuring that the driver could clearly see the road ahead. *L. Nixon.*

Class 31 31115 at Barkston East Junction box with a Summer Saturdays only King's Cross-Skegness train on 9th July, 1983. The Brush Type 2s, as they were originally known, were introduced way back in 1957. This particular locomotive started life as D5533 and is one of the examples of the class that is still with us today. *L. Nixon.*

THE ENGINE SHED

The exact date of the opening of the GN locomotive and carriage shed that stood adjacent to Grantham station is unclear but they were in use by late 1855. The building consisted of two single-ended, brick-built sheds adjoining each other. Each was 172ft long and had two roads with arched entrances. The Ambergate Company's single-road engine shed, which was located at the Canal Yard station site, closed when the GN facility came into operation.

A total of 37 locomotives were shedded at Grantham by 1889 but there was room for only ten under cover. Patrick Stirling proposed a shed extension which would accommodate a further ten engines under cover. He made the case that if the shed were extended it would enable the GNR to run trains to York and Leeds with only one stop. The resulting work was limited to the original two-road engine shed being extended by a mere 10ft at the rear. It was made into a through building with both tracks extended for 85ft to buffer-stops. At the same time the turntable was moved from beside the shed to a less-restricted location at the extreme top end of the yard. The space made available was given over to a set of shear legs.

In October 1896 it was decided to build a new engine shed at the south end of the site. The building was to house twenty engines, with the possibility of extension for a further twenty. The four-road single-ended shed was completed in 1897 and its east wall was constructed in corrugated iron in anticipation of the extension. A second turntable was installed, 52ft in diameter, at the southwest corner of the new building. The ground set aside for the future extension was used for coal stacking and the enlargement was never effected.

The District Locomotive Superintendent had three outstations in his remit - Sleaford, Leicester and Newark. Leicester opened in 1882 and was transferred to Colwick during the World War 1 period. Sleaford opened in 1883 with two engines and four sets of men. These arrangements continued until Sleaford became the responsibility of Boston in September 1930. Even so, Grantham sent a crew by train to work the middle-pilot shift at Sleaford. Newark came under Grantham in 1912 when it was transferred from Retford. Under the LNER, Grantham District was abolished and outstations were transferred to Peterborough District.

As well as providing crews for express workings to King's Cross, Leeds, York, and Newcastle, Grantham also worked local passenger and freight services to Nottingham, Lincoln and Boston. The shed also had the exclusive working of the High Dyke to Stainby ironstone branch within its remit.

After renewals in the 1930s the 70ft turntable was removed in 1951 and

These two views taken from the top of the coaling plant in 1935, clearly show the layout of Grantham Motive Power Depot. Above, looking north, with the original engine/carriage shed and Grantham station in the background and below, looking south, with the 'New' single-ended shed, with its original 'North-light' roof, the coal stacks are both sides of the line to the left of the shed. A number of Class C12 4-4-2Ts can be seen stabled on the ash pit line. Eleven C12s were allocated at Grantham shed at some point during their lifetime. *R. K. Blencowe.*

replaced by the locally-famous turning triangle which was laid on open ground between the two sheds. There was not sufficient space to layout a conventional triangle so the two approach roads crossed by means of a scissors crossing - an application which was unique on British railways.

In 1955 the north light roof of the 'new' shed was replaced with a new structure formed of asbestos sheeting on a steel frame. By 1960 the gable roof of the old shed had deteriorated to such a degree that the building had been abandoned and the decision was made to demolish it after some 105 year's of service.

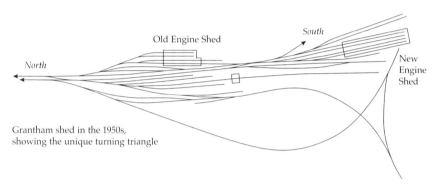

Old Engine Shed

South

North

New
Engine
Shed

Grantham shed in the 1950s,
showing the unique turning triangle

Grantham-based A4 Pacific 60014 'Silver Link' in the shed yard in May 1950. The A4's were the ultimate in power, speed and grace and were the pride of the Gresley-designed fleet. 60014 was the first A4 to pull the 'Silver Jubilee' train, making the inaugural journey from King's Cross in its silver and grey livery on 27th September, 1935. It was withdrawn from 'Top Shed' on 29th December, 1962 and languished at Doncaster Works until 7th September, 1963, when it was broken up for scrap. *A. J. Ludlam collection.*

The 'New' shed pictured on 5th August, 1963, with Class B1 4-6-0 61272 in the foreground. The locomotive was condemned in January 1965 but survived a little longer as Departmental Stationary Boiler No. 25. *F. A. Blencowe.*

Colwick-based Class O2/1 2-8-0 63923 parked under the shear legs at the side of the 'New' shed on 5th August, 1963. *F. A. Blencowe.*

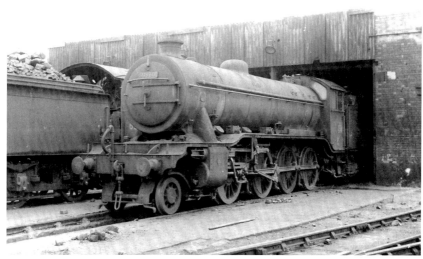

Grantham Class 02/3 2-8-0 63960 outside the rather dilapidated 'New' shed building on 5th August, 1963, shortly before closure. *F. A. Blencowe.*

Three Class A3 Pacifics in Grantham shed yard on 5th August, 1963, 60108 'Gay Crusader', 60054 'Prince of Wales' and 60048 'Doncaster', all fitted with German smoke deflectors. 60108 and 60048 were withdrawn soon after this photograph was taken. 60054 survived until June 1964, when it was scrapped at Kings, Norwich. *F. A. Blencowe.*

Class A3 Pacific 60056 'Centenary' at Grantham shed on 28th April, 1962. *R. Heppenstall/D. Enefer.*

Ivatt 4-4-0 Class D3, originally D4, 62000 outside the old shed. This loco was converted into the LNER Officers saloon engine after a number of runs were disrupted by engine failures during the war. Originally built in 1897 as GNR class D2 engine, 1075 was one of a class which was intended by Ivatt for secondary usage. After the turn of the century, they were often used to pilot Stirling singles on the heavier expresses. Before the First World War, four of this type were shedded at Grantham, after Grouping they spent most of their time on the country workings not least Nottingham, Grantham and Newark. From Grouping, 1075 was shedded in numerous areas, including Darlington after 1931, and then returned to the Southern area working from New England and Boston, after 1937. 62000, as it became in 1948, was rebuilt in 1944 with the more modern cab that this picture shows. It was then most frequently based at Grantham, and finally withdrawn in 1951. *H. C. Casserley/A. J. Ludlam collection.*

Gateshead Class A2 Pacific 60518 'Tehran', locally-based Class A1 Pacific 60144 'King's Courier' and York Class V2 2-6-2 60974 head the line-up at the 'New' shed in May 1956. *J. Champion/R. K. Blencowe.*

Grantham-based Class A3 Pacific 60063 'Isinglass' under the coaling plant on 19th April, 1957. She was built at Doncaster in June 1925 as LNER Class A1 No. 2562, and was withdrawn in June 1964. *R. Heppenstall/D. Enefer.*

Peppercorn Class A1 Pacific 60149 'Amadis' in Grantham shed yard on 19th April, 1957 while allocated to King's Cross depot. She was built at Darlington Works in May 1949 and was scrapped just fifteen years later in June 1964. *R. Heppenstall/D. Enefer.*

Grantham-based Class B1 4-6-0 61251 'Oliver Bury' in the shed yard on 5th August, 1963. 61251 was one of the Eastern Region examples that took part in the 1948 Locomotive Exchange Trials, working on the South Devon and Midland Main Lines. *F. A. Blencowe.*

The new order: National Express East Coast Class 91 91117 arrives at Grantham's Platform 2 with a northbound express on 25th September 2008. *P. Eldridge.*

East Midlands Trains Class 153 153308 and Class 158 158865 wait at Platform 4 with the 11.45 service from Skegness to Nottingham on 2nd August, 2018. *P. Eldridge.*

Hull Trains Class 180 'Adelante' 180109 arrives at Grantham with the 1400 service for King's Cross on 2nd August, 2018. *P. Eldridge.*

GBRF Class 66 66719 'Metro-Land' heads north through Grantham with a loaded Middleton Towers – Monk Bretton sand train on 2nd August, 2018. *P. Eldridge.*

BELTON PARK MILITARY RAILWAY

During World War 1 there were many military training camps within the GNR area. One of the most important was at Belton Park, near Grantham. Originally the railhead for the camp was at Grantham station but this was four miles away from the camp and not convenient. In 1916 a $4^{1}/_{2}$ mile single-track railway was built to serve the camp. A junction was formed with the East Coast main line at a point half-a-mile south of Peascliffe tunnel. A signal box was built to control the junction, which gave access to the military railway.

The military railway left the sidings and crossed Belton Lane on the level, then turned immediately eastwards to run parallel to the lane. It crossed the A607 road and entered Belton Park. There it turned sharply north and terminated in a reversing spur. There were no run-round facilities at the spur so trains were propelled away from it. The reversing spur was necessary as the River Witham ran through the park in a small valley and the railway had to descend to the valley bottom in order to cross the river which it did by virtue of a low bridge. The line then skirted the southern edge of Belton Park serving a number of regimental headquarters in Alma Park. This section ended in another reversing spur from which the line headed southwards on a slightly rising gradient to what was then the outskirts of Grantham. It crossed Hanowby Lane to serve a military hospital nearby.

The line was worked by War Department locomotives and military personnel. There was a trip between the exchange sidings and Grantham goods yard each morning and afternoon. War Department locomotives were occasionally used on these trips, running through to and from Grantham. After the end of World War 1 Belton Park camp was run-down, the railway track was removed, and it was put up for sale in January 1922, the junction signal box closing in May of that year.

A Manning Wardle 0-4-0ST hauls three open wagons over a section of the Belton Park Military Railway, circa 1917. *A. J. Ludlam collection.*

Ex GNR Howlden 45ft carriage. Positioned in the 'UP yard' at Grantham, this carriage was one of the 45ft non-corridor style express carriages introduced by E. F. Howlden from 1898. Built at Doncaster, they were companions to the Clerestory carriages being built for the ECJS as well as GNR stock contemporaneously. The carriage is in Departmental stock livery and has been converted from what is believed to be a Dia 129 Luggage, Toilet Composite. Although the interior of the carriage was often modified, they rarely changed the exterior. Amongst uses were for breakdown trains which often spent a long time waiting, hence the use of 'life expired' carriages such as this 50 year old, when photographed, rather than more modern stock. It is likely that it is one of two which were withdrawn in 1965, either a Tool van, or Signal and Telegraph van.
From the Great Northern Railway Society's collection.

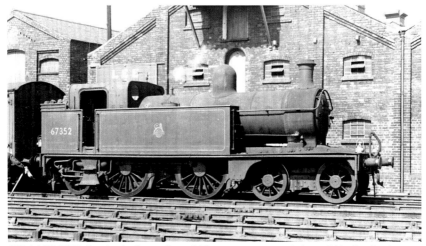

C12 4-4-2T 67352 shunting in the goods yard. There were many variations within the class but one in particular is evident in this loco: it has square ends to the tanks. *P. M. Groom/P. Craig collection.*

GRANTHAM'S SIGNAL BOXES

Grantham was ideally suited as a place where steam engines were changed on passenger trains, it being slightly more than halfway between London and York, but having the important junction to Nottingham nearby.

Despite a lack of photographic evidence, it seems clear that there would have been a kind of signal station at the junction, as well as one within the station to control the movement of locomotives being changed. These were not the kind of signal boxes that were still to be viewed at the end of steam in 1968, rather they appear to have been open towers, having little covered accommodation for the staff.

In the early years, trains were controlled by slotted post signals which had three positions, including 'caution', but they were not very safe during the winter when snow often stopped them working properly. There was a tower at Grantham Junction, but at that time, the trains ran on an 'interval' basis, since interlocking between signals and points or switches had not been invented.

By 1868, a new Grantham Junction signal box had been built using interlocking alongside electric block telegraph working, although this was to control the nearby Gonerby tunnel.

After a number of collisions on the railways, including two at Welwyn and Abbots Ripton on the GNR itself, The Board of Trade, that part of the government which oversaw railway safety, demanded that safety was improved. This resulted in the installation of electric block telegraph along the whole main line in 1872.

Traffic into and through Grantham had by 1874 become so extensive, it was necessary to open three new, more modern, signal boxes. These were Grantham North, South and the Yard box. They all operated the first interlocked signalling installation at the station. Later in the decade, a means of allowing the signal men to communicate with each other by a modified form of Morse Code and a telegraph instrument were installed. By the end of the decade, the signals became two-position after the 'caution' position was abolished.

By 1881, traffic through and around Grantham had grown to such a level that new boxes had to be built. By this time the more modern style, which lasted until the 1970's, had a ground floor which contained the mechanical equipment whilst the top had the lever frames and generally a fire for the signal men, who now worked in shifts over the 24 hour period. Whilst the North box was enlarged, the junction to Nottingham was rebuilt, which meant that the Grantham Junction Signal Box was replaced by another box at Barrowby Road, further north. These new boxes contained equipment that made it impossible to set signal and point levers to conflicting routes. The upper floor had windows and a narrow balcony to allow for cleaning, as well as providing a place to signal by flag or lamp.

By 1881 the re-signalling had taken place using the characteristic Somersault signals, with which the GNR became synonymous. These lasted in many places until the introduction of electric colour signals during BR times.

After 1895, the signalling and control at Grantham basically remained the same until the end of steam, although after grouping, electric track circuits were installed to allow colour signalling in the 1930's, which permitted the 'Streamliner' trains to run at high speed.

All four of the boxes within the Grantham area were closed between 1968 and 1971, although the Yard box was converted to a new design of box until the Doncaster Power Box came into use in 1980, thus allowing the HSTs to run at the projected speeds of 125 mph.

Grantham Yard Signal Box. From the beginning of the GNR, Grantham was the first station along the GNR, later East Coast Main Line, that was used for changing engines on expresses to the North and even Scotland. Because of this, it needed more than the usual signal box at each end of the station, and so in 1872, this box was built at the end of the platform to control the yard. Initially it had a 30 lever frame, but within five years this was expanded to 50. This box controlled the movement of the engines that were taken off incoming expresses, and also those that replaced them. It was in service with this role until the 1970's then whilst BR completed the change over to power signal boxes it stayed as a fringe box of the Doncaster and Peterborough boxes until the 1980's when it was finally closed. The picture shows it in BR times, but apart from moving the operating frames from the front of the box to the rear, it was externally pretty much as originally built and used by the GNR and later the LNER. *From the Great Northern Railway Society's collection.*

MEMORIES OF ALLINGTON JUNCTION

George Newcomb was born on 14th September 1917. Some time later his father took up the position of signalman at Allington Junction box having moved from High Dyke, he was there until 1926. Some of George's earliest recollections are of when the family lived at the road crossing Gate House.

Allington Junction is situated on the Nottingham to Grantham railway at the point where there is a junction leading to Barkston and on to Sleaford and the East Coast. The railway here is crossed by a lane leading from the Nottingham to Grantham road and in those days it led to two farms on the other side of the line and continued as a bridle road to Allington. The railway is on a slight embankment and, as the crossing was made by a level crossing with gates opened from the signal box, the lane had a slight embankment from the normal level. There were four houses on the main road side of the crossing, one of which was occupied by my grandparents.

The lane was a dirt road covered in granite chips and had a wide grass verge on each side and a considerable number of trees between the main road and the level crossing.

As you stood at the level crossing and looked southwards towards Grantham a hill rose to Great Gonerby and a footpath ran from the rear of the signal box, under the Barkston line, and proceeded past Tinkler's farm up the hill, through a covert to the village.

The railway ran towards Nottingham and about a mile from the junction box was Sedgebrook station. There was very little road traffic to use the level crossing. An exciting event was the occasional annual visit of the steam driven cultivators and threshing machines, which were to arrive with two steam traction engines, the ploughs and wooden caravan for the operatives.

A considerable number of trains seemed to run on the line and I well remember looking to see if they had GNR or LNER painted on their tenders as this was the time of regrouping. Passenger locos were a very bright green and goods engines black. In the summer enormous numbers of excursion trains fully packed used to pass by on

An early photograph of George Newcomb's father pictured in the sidecar of the motorbike, with Allington Junction signal box in the background.

their way from Nottingham to Skegness and of course they proceeded through the junction down the link line to Barkston.

Three signalmen ran the signal box on shifts during the week and at weekends, as we lived in the gatehouse, father had to remain at home to open the gates for any road traffic. When we were taken to Grantham to go shopping we always walked up the railway track to Sedgebrook station and caught the train there. We were always told to be careful when we walked because of wagon grease from the axle boxes being on the track. I was intrigued by the gas lights on the trains, all non-corridor, which came on when we went through the tunnel before reaching Grantham.

The Gatehouse at Barrowby Vale consisted of two downstairs rooms with a pantry and three bedrooms. Water was supplied by a pump in the yard, which had about eight steps leading to the back door as the house was built on the level of the railway. Lighting was by paraffin lamp and candles. The living room had windows facing onto the railway and down the garden towards Grantham. Here at five o'clock you would see Grandfather come home from work from the link line where he was foreman platelayer. He always carried his large hammer (used for driving in wooden keys into the line chairs) over his shoulder with his bag of tools hanging from it and he usually wore a red muffler. The other downstairs room had a bay window facing the railway and another window looked onto the lane and across the county to Belvoir. If you could see the castle you knew it would be a fine day!

Allington Junction signal box and Gatehouse pictured in 1997. *T. Newcomb.*

40

COAL TRAINS

As well as being a local passenger route, the Nottingham line was also very important for the movement of coal. Huge quantities were brought to Grantham from the coalfields of Nottinghamshire and Derbyshire. From Grantham it was progressed via the slow line to the marshalling yards at Peterborough, and from there to London and the southern counties.

These very heavy, slow-moving, loose-coupled trains entered Grantham from Barrowby Road on the down side of the main line. They then had to cross both main lines in order to reach the up slow line. Two routes were used to achieve this, firstly by using the cross-over near Grantham North signal box, then moving through the station along the up main line, and then switching on to the up slow line near the South Box. The alternative was that they could keep on the down side by using the lock & block two-way slow road that ran between the station and the engine shed, after which they would take the south cross-over. In the early days the coal trains were quite often stopped at Barrowby Road for the engine to take water. Once a main-line path was available they would move over North Box crossing and on through the station, giving them a good run at Stoke Bank.

Colwick Class 01 2-8-0 63768 with an up coal train at Little Ponton in September, 1962. *L. Nixon.*

Class A3 Pacific 60107 'Royal Lancer' at the north end of Grantham station with a down express in 1959. At this time it was allocated to Grantham shed. It was scrapped at Doncaster works in September 1963. *R. K. Blencowe.*

Andrew Barclay 0-6-0ST 'Sewstern' busy shunting loaded wagons near Stainby on 27th March, 1964. Once made into trainloads, they would be worked to the exchange sidings at High Dyke. *M. Mensing.*

IRON ORE TRAFFIC

To the south west of Grantham there was a network of lines facilitating the movement of iron-ore from quarries in the area. One of them left the East Coast main line at High Dyke, half-a-mile south of Stoke tunnel. There were exchange sidings at High Dyke from where the line ran on a stiff gradient to Colsterworth. The High Dyke line opened in 1916 and was soon extended to Stainby. In 1925 it was extended a further three miles from the Skillington Junction with the Stainby line to Sproxton.

In 1935 the output of the branch was such that there were eleven trains each-way daily. They were assembled at High Dyke into three daily trains to Frodingham, two to Colwick, and one Parkgate, all via Grantham, and by 1938 the number had risen to fifteen. The wartime demand for steel required more trains, which resulted in four to Frodingham and one each to Parkgate, Scotland, and Tees-side. There were two trains to Frodingham and another if required, to Tees-side on Sundays.

Heavy goods engines were based at Grantham to deal with the iron-ore traffic. In the late 1920s ex-GCR Class 'O4' 2-8-0s arrived, and they remained until being replaced by twelve Class 'O1' 2-8-0s which within two years were replaced by Class 'O2' 2-8-0s, seventeen of which were still at Grantham in 1945. During the 1945-50 period the 'O2s' were assisted on the High Dyke traffic by some of the last remaining ex-GCR 'Q4' class 0-8-0s, eight of which were at Grantham at nationalisation.

Grantham-based Class 02/4 2-8-0 63930 climbing towards Colsterworth with a train of empties on the mineral line from High Dyke to Stainby on 25th June, 1960. In total, 67 O2's were built by the GNR and LNER. All survived into Nationalisation but the prototype No. 3921 was withdrawn in 1948. Four locomotives were scrapped in 1960 and the rate of withdrawals accelerated with the last 40 being taken out of service in 1963. *H. Ballantyne.*

York-based Class A2/3 Pacific 60524 'Herringbone' with an up express at Grantham in 1959. 60524 was built in October 1947 and was pensioned-off in January 1965. *R. K. Blencowe.*

The north end of Grantham station in 1959 with plenty of spotters in view as Copley Hill Class A1 Pacific 60131 'Osprey' awaits to depart with a down express in 1959. The locomotive met its maker on 4th October, 1965. *R. K. Blencowe.*

Merchant Navy Class 4-6-2 35019 'French Line CGT' attracts a lot of attention as it waits at Grantham station while working on the Eastern Region during the 1948 loco exchanges. It is paired with an ex-LMS tender with a water scoop fitted. These were not required on the Southern Region as there were no water troughs. *G. F. Gillford.*

Gateshead Class A3 Pacific 60078 'Night Hawk' approaches Grantham station on a down mixed freight in 1959. 60078 was withdrawn in October, 1962. *R. K. Blencowe.*

In the late 1950's Colwick K3 2-6-0 61821 works mineral wagons through Grantham station. These could well be iron ore empties returning from Scunthorpe to High Dyke. The Gresley three-cylinder K3's were instantly recognisable by their large, 6ft diameter boilers. 61821 was withdrawn on 16th September, 1962 and was broken up at Cashmores, Great Bridge. *A. J. Ludlam collection.*

A4 Pacific 60029 'Woodcock' departs from Grantham with an up express on 16th May, 1963. Built at Doncaster Works in July 1937 as LNER No. 4493, she was withdrawn from New England shed in October, 1963. *K. C. H. Fairey.*

CONCLUSION

Grantham enginemen had a fine reputation for reliability and good timekeeping and both the shed and the station were major sources of local employment over the years.

The introduction of diesel power in the form of the 3,300hp 'Deltics' in 1961 meant that the days of the Gresley Pacifics were numbered. The time-honoured practice of engine-changing became unnecessary and so there was no good reason to keep Grantham engine shed open. At end of the 1963 summer timetable, on the 9th September, the shed closed and most of the serviceable locomotives were transferred to Doncaster. 18 drivers, 21 firemen and 21 cleaners were made redundant, however 63 drivers and 53 firemen were retained and were accommodated in the buildings at the south end of the Up platform. The shed buildings and tracks remained in situ a little longer to provide temporary shelter for DMUs during the harsh winter of 1963/64. Clearance of the servicing structure began in March 1964, the work took some time and it was not until November when the coaling tower was demolished by explosives.

Compared to the rest of Lincolnshire, Grantham has been relatively unaffected by line closures. The Leicester service finished in 1953 and the line via Honington to Lincoln Central went in 1965, despite having been recommended for retention as a useful diversionary route in the Beeching Report of 1963, the Newark route being retained in its place. In the mid-1980s much of the station was rebuilt and modernised.

In 2005 Barkston South Junction–Barkston East Junction was removed when a new chord was built at Allington Junction to allow Skegness services to access Grantham station without having to cross over the main lines.

Motive power continued to evolve. The Deltics were, in turn, replaced by the InterCity High Speed Trains in 1978, one of which was to later set a new world record for a diesel train of 148mph while descending Stoke Bank on a test run on 1st November, 1987. Following the completion of the East Coast Main Line electrification many of these HSTs were superseded by a new generation of InterCity 225 electric trains.

Today Grantham continues to be an important rail hub, with direct cross-country services to Liverpool, Norwich, Manchester, Sheffield, Nottingham and Skegness. The East Coast main line services north to York, Leeds and Hull, and south to Peterborough and Kings Cross remain, but are not quite as exciting as when the cream of GNR, LNER and BR steam locomotives were in charge.

Colwick-based Thompson Class L1 2-6-4T 67780 stands at Grantham station in 1962. 100 of these attractive, 2-cylinder engines were built between 1946 and 1950 but they had very short lives. Withdrawals began in 1960 and by the end of 1962 the class was extinct. 67780 was taken out of service on 29th December that year and was scrapped at Darlington works.

Steam was still to be seen in the Grantham area in 1964. Colwick-based Thompson B1 4-6-0 61281 is seen here with a returning Summer Saturday train from the Lincolnshire coast on the Grantham to Nottingham line in August of that year. The loco survived until February 1966 when it was sold for scrap to Birds of Long Marston. *G. Siviour.*